# Just Watch Me!

Ron Benson
Lynn Bryan
Kim Newlove
Liz Stenson
Iris Zammit

**CONSULTANTS**
Lillian Blakey
Florence Brown
Estella Clayton
Kathyrn D'Angelo
Susan Elliott-Johns
Charolette Player
Shari Schwartz
Lynn Swanson
Helen Tomassini
Debbie Toope

**Prentice Hall Ginn**

# Contents

**Puppet Parade**   3
factual recount by
Nancy Davidson

**Jenny the Juvenile Juggler**   11
poem by Dennis Lee

**The Great Austini**   14
story by Wendy Lewis

**The Comedy Club**   21
television script by Liz Stenson

**A Visit with Barbara Reid**   27
interview

**Daniel's Writing**
advertisement

# Puppet Parade

by Nancy Davidson
Puppets by Laurie Stein
Photographed by Ray Boudreau

Welcome to our puppet parade!
We have a sock puppet, a shadow puppet, and a glove puppet.
We made them all! Here's how.

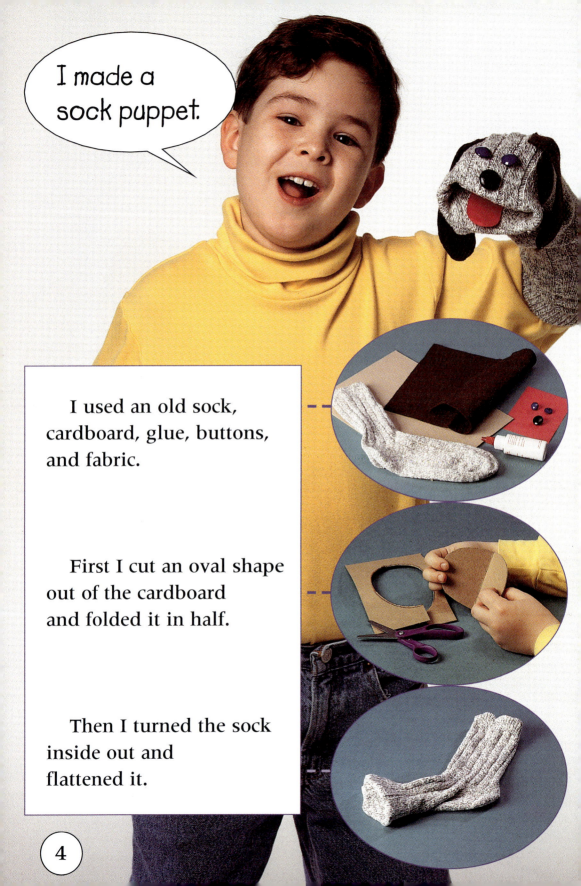

"I made a sock puppet."

I used an old sock, cardboard, glue, buttons, and fabric.

First I cut an oval shape out of the cardboard and folded it in half.

Then I turned the sock inside out and flattened it.

I spread glue all over the inside of the cardboard and placed the toe inside the fold.

I let the glue dry, turned the sock the right side out, and pulled it over the cardboard. This gave my puppet a happy mouth.

I used buttons for eyes, felt to make the ears, and red paper for his tongue. I used a shiny black button for his wet nose.

**Presenting Benny Beagle!**

I made a shadow puppet.

I used thin cardboard, two drinking straws (the kind that can bend), a paper fastener, and tape.

First I drew an outline of a shark's body on the cardboard and cut it out. I poked a hole at the bottom of the jaw.

Next I drew the shark's bottom jaw and cut it out. I poked a hole in the end.

Then I placed the two holes on top of each other and pushed a paper fastener through them.

Last of all I taped one of the bent straws to the body and one to the bottom jaw. Now my puppet can snap her jaws!

**Presenting Shelly Shark!**

"I made a glove puppet."

I used newspaper, one nylon knee sock, thin cardboard, yarn, fabric, glue, masking tape, sequins, and a felt pen.

**First I made the head.**
1. I squashed one sheet of newspaper into a ball and wrapped it inside another sheet of newspaper.

2. I pushed the ball down into the toe of the sock and pulled the leg up to my elbow.

3. I twisted the ball around once, and pulled the sock down over my hand and over the ball.

4. I put the sock back on my arm and kept pulling it down and over the ball until all the sock was used.

5. I cut a piece of cardboard 15 cm by 10 cm and rolled it into a tube just big enough for my finger.

6. I made a hole in the head, put some glue in it, and attached the tube. Then I tied the loose ends.

7. I made a mouth and nose from felt, eyes with a felt pen, and hair from the yarn. I glued them on to my puppet's face.

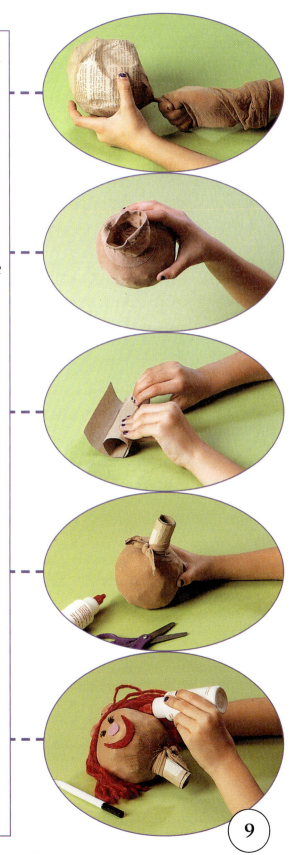

**Next I made the body.**

8. I made a paper pattern and used it to cut two shapes out of the fabric. I glued the edges together but left the neck and the holes for the arms open.

9. I cut hands out of cardboard, squeezed glue in the neck and arm holes, and attached the head and the hands.

Last of all, I added sequins to my puppet's dress.

**Presenting Princess Polly!**

On with the parade!

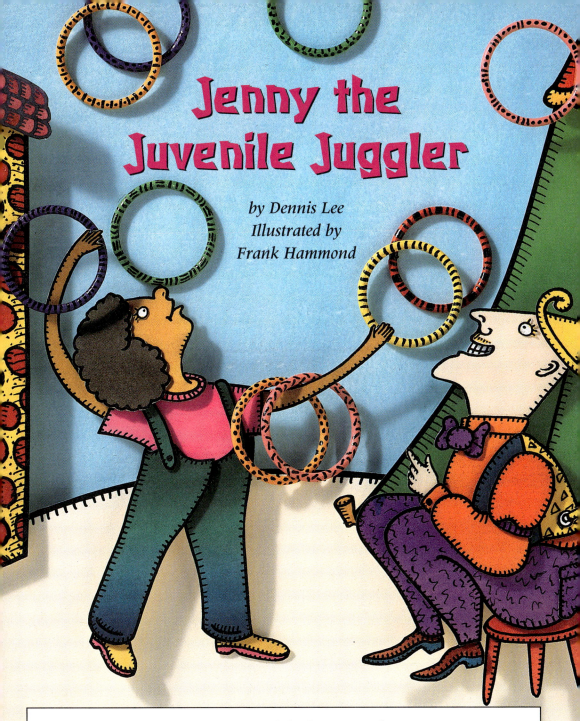

# Jenny the Juvenile Juggler

by Dennis Lee
Illustrated by Frank Hammond

Jenny had hoops she could sling in the air
And she brought them along to the Summerhill Fair.
And a man from a carnival sideshow was there,
Who declared that he needed a juggler.

And it's,
  Oops! Jenny, whoops! Jenny,
  Swing along your hoops, Jenny,
  Spin a little pattern as you go;
Because it's
  Oops! Jenny's hoops! Jenny,
  Sling a loop-the-loop, Jenny,
  Whoops! Jenny, oops! Jenny, O!

Well the man was astonished at how the hoops flew,
And he said, "It's amazing what some kids can do!"
And now at the carnival, Act Number Two
Is Jenny the Juvenile Juggler.

**And it's,**
>   Oops! Jenny, whoops! Jenny,
>   Swing along your hoops, Jenny,
>   Spin a little pattern as you go;

**Because it's**
>   Oops! Jenny's hoops! Jenny,
>   Sling a loop-the-loop, Jenny,
>   Whoops! Jenny, oops! Jenny, O!

# The Great Austini

by Wendy Lewis
Illustrated by Anne Villeneuve

Every summer we have a party on my street. We have balloons and games and good things to eat. Dad always puts on his magic show. It's the same thing every year. Most of the kids on my street have seen Dad's magic show a zillion times, except Austin, the new kid next door. He seems a bit shy.

While the rest of us played tag, Austin sat with the grown-ups and babies. But he was watching us.

"Come eat with us," I said. "It's boring with the grown-ups."

"OK," said Austin.

I introduced him to my friends. Then we stuffed ourselves. Paul ate three cheeseburgers. Gina ate a plateful of pickles. I ate four scoops of ice cream—all different colours. This is the only time our parents let us eat whatever we want.

"Time for the magic show!" called my mom.

Austin's eyes lit up. "Magic show?"

"Yes," I said. "Do you like magic?"

"I sure do!" said Austin.

   Everyone pulled up lawn chairs in front of the table where Dad performs. Austin, Jenny, Paul, and I sat in the front row.

   I stood up to introduce my dad. I always do.

   "Ladies and gentlemen, please let's hear it for the Great Garbeenzi!"

   Everyone clapped loudly. They love my dad. He ran out from behind a bush with his top hat in his hand.

   "Thank you!" said the Great Garbeenzi. "Please, enough applause. You're too kind!"

    Then he asked for a volunteer to help with his first trick. Ten hands went up. Dad's eyes wandered over the crowd, and stopped at Austin, who had not raised his hand.

    "How about you, Austin?" said Dad.

    Austin turned bright red and shook his head.

    "All right, then . . . the Great Garbeenzi calls . . . Gina!"

    "Dad didn't mean to embarrass you," I whispered to Austin.

    "It's OK," he whispered back.

We watched the Great Garbeenzi perform trick after trick. He made rings mysteriously link together. He made a scarf mysteriously grow bigger and bigger. People clapped every time. They really love my dad.

Whenever the Great Garbeenzi asked for a new volunteer, I saw Austin's hand move. It was as if he wanted to volunteer, but was still too shy.

"If you want, I'll go with you," I whispered.

"OK," said Austin.

I jumped up. "This time, the Great Garbeenzi has a special new assistant. Ladies and gentlemen, let's have some applause for the Great Austini!"

Austin grinned and bowed. Everyone clapped.

Austin's job was to stick his finger into a glass of magic water. His finger seemed to disappear. We'd all seen the trick before, but this time something different happened . . . something SCARY! Austin screamed and snatched his hand back. His finger reappeared, but something was wrong with it. It was sticking out in a very strange way. Dad looked scared. People rushed up to see Austin's hand.

"Fear not!" he said. "The Great Austini's finger is fine!" He held up his hand for all to see. Now it looked normal.

"How did you do that?" I asked.

"I'm double-jointed," Austin whispered. "I can do all sorts of tricks with my fingers."

As people crowded around Austin, laughing and patting him on the back, my dad called, "How would the Great Austini like to be the Great Garbeenzi's assistant from now on?"

The smile on Austin's face was pure magic.

# The Comedy Club
## A Television Show

*by Liz Stenson*
*Illustrated by Albert Molnar*

**ANNOUNCER:** Welcome, boys and girls, to The Comedy Club! This is half an hour of fun and entertainment for all. We are sure you will enjoy our jokes and skits. Now here is our first skit, The Rope Joke! It stars the great trio Eeny, Meeny, and Mo! Don't laugh too much!

(EENY *and* MEENY *are laughing together. They listen for a minute, then laugh again.* MO *moves closer, trying to hear.*)

- **MO:** Why are you laughing?
- **EENY:** We're telling jokes.
- **MO:** I like jokes.
- **EENY:** We like jokes, too.
- **MO:** Did you hear the rope joke?
- **EENY:** No, I don't know that one.
- **MEENY:** Let's hear this rope joke.
- **MO:** Skip it!

(AUDIENCE *cheers and applauds.*)

**ANNOUNCER:** And now a word from our sponsor, Scrubby Soap.

**COMMERCIAL ANNOUNCER:**
 Try Scrubby Soap.
 It scrubs kids like
 no other soap in the world!
**SINGING VOICES:**
 Scrub their ears and scrub their noses,
 Scrub their elbows, scrub their toeses!
 Scrub their necks, and scrub their faces,
 Scrub in all the dirty places!
 Scrub, scrub, Scrubby Soap!

**ANNOUNCER:** And now back to the show. Our next joke stars Milly and the pet store owner.

(MILLY is *walking back and forth, looking in the cages.*)
**STORE OWNER:** Hello.
 May I help you?
**MILLY:** I want to buy a rabbit.
 How much are they?
**STORE OWNER:** Fifteen dollars apiece.
**MILLY:** Fifteen dollars *a piece?*
**STORE OWNER:** That's the price.
**MILLY:** But I want to buy a whole rabbit, not just a piece!

(AUDIENCE *cheers and applauds.*)

**ANNOUNCER:** You are going to love our next skit. It stars that crazy pair, Flip and Flap.

**FLIP:** Hi, Flap.
**FLAP:** Hi, Flip.
**FLIP:** I have a question for you.
**FLAP:** What?
**FLIP:** If I caught a fly and put it in a pail of maple syrup, how would it get out?
**FLAP:** I don't know. I'm stuck.
**FLIP:** So is the fly!

**AUDIENCE:** Ahhhhhhhhhhhhh!

**ANNOUNCER:** And now a short break while we bring you this message from Crunchy Munchy, the fantastic new cereal all kids love!

**COMMERCIAL ANNOUNCER:** Girls and boys! Have you tried Crunchy Munchy? This cereal is amazing! It will make you strong!
It will make you run like the wind!
It will make you jump like a tiger!
Crunchy Munchy will even prevent cavities!
There is nothing quite like Crunchy Munchy!
Buy a box today!

**ANNOUNCER:** Welcome back to the show. Our next skit stars Little Bo Peep and Little Boy Blue.

(BO *is crying.*)

**BLUE:** Oh, don't cry, Bo.
**BO:** But I lost my sheep.
**BLUE:** Maybe they're in the meadow.
**BO:** I looked there already. They're lost for sure.
**BLUE:** Did you put an ad in the Lost and Found?
**BO:** That wouldn't do a bit of good.
**BLUE:** Why not?
**BO:** My sheep can't read!

(AUDIENCE *cheers and applauds.*)

**ANNOUNCER:** That's it, boys and girls. We've come to the end of this week's show! I hope you enjoyed The Comedy Club. Don't forget to tune in next week for more fun and laughs! See you then!

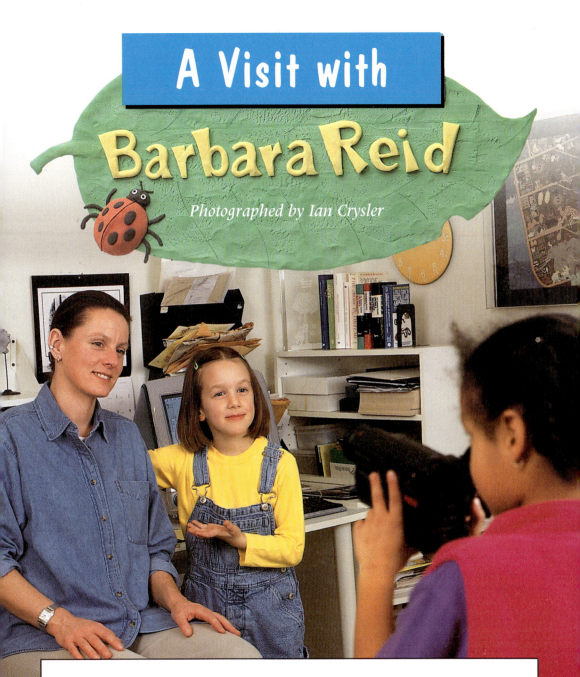

# A Visit with Barbara Reid

*Photographed by Ian Crysler*

**CAITLIN:** We're here in Barbara Reid's studio. Barbara is the author and illustrator of many children's books. She is known especially for her Plasticine illustrations.

CAITLIN: Barbara, why did you become an illustrator?

BARBARA: I like to draw and I enjoy making pictures to tell a story. I have enjoyed doing that since I was really little.

CAITLIN: How did you learn to do story illustrations?

BARBARA: I went to art school, where I learned to draw and paint. I learned to use Plasticine by playing around with it for a long, long time.

CAITLIN: Which do you like best—writing or illustrating?

BARBARA: I like illustrating because it's easier for me.

CAITLIN: Where do you work?

BARBARA: Here in my studio. You can see my desk and the countertops for spreading out my pictures. These are the big tubs to hold the Plasticine. I have lots of books too. When I want to make a picture, perhaps of a butterfly, I can find out exactly what it looks like.

CAITLIN: Where do you get all those colours?

BARBARA: I mix the colours. I take two small blobs, each a different colour, and I mix them together with my hands, squishing and squishing until they blend into one colour.

CAITLIN: Why do you especially like to use Plasticine?
BARBARA: I like Plasticine because I can keep changing things as I work. If I make a face that's not quite right, I just take it off and do it again.

CAITLIN: What is the most difficult part?
BARBARA: Eyes are the most difficult. It's hard to get the expression right.

CAITLIN: How do you begin to illustrate a book?
BARBARA: First I read the story and imagine the pictures in my head. Next I draw them on paper. Then I take a piece of heavy cardboard and make a background with Plasticine.

CAITLIN: How do you make the background?

BARBARA: Let me show you. I'll make an underwater picture. First I take a blob of Plasticine and spread it out with my thumbs. The Plasticine needs to be about as thick as the peanut butter in a sandwich. I don't worry if it's not too smooth. Then I take another colour, perhaps green, smear some wiggly lines across the blue background, and rub them in with my thumb.

CAITLIN: Your thumbs must get sore!

BARBARA: Yes, sometimes they get very sore.

CAITLIN: What's the next step?

BARBARA: I put on the second layer. I'll make some fish to put on top of the background, and maybe some seaweed.

CAITLIN: Now what will you do?
BARBARA: For the next layer, I'll add little details, like bubbles.

CAITLIN: Which of your books is your favourite?
BARBARA: I guess my favourite is the next book I'll be doing. I enjoy imagining the pictures, but often my hands don't make the pictures as exciting as the one I imagine.

CAITLIN: Your illustrations and your books are all exciting. I'm looking forward to reading your next book!
BARBARA: Thanks, Caitlin.
CAITLIN: Thank *you*, Barbara.